BOOK 1 Listen Up, Talk Back

JN061744

Gillian Flaherty, James Bean, and Yoshihito Kamakura

Published and distributed by Seibido Publishing Co., Ltd.

Created and developed by
International Language Teaching Services Ltd
First floor, 1 Market Street
Saffron Walden, Essex CB10 1JB, UK

help@ilts.info
www.ilts.info

First published 2019

Editor: James Bean
Illustrations:
Cover and text design: Clare Webber www.clarewebber.co.uk
Photographs: Shutterstock, Bigstock

ISBN 978-4-7919-7204-3

音声ファイルのダウンロード/ストリーミング

CD マーク表示がある箇所は、音声を弊社 HP より無料でダウンロード/ストリーミングすることができます。トップページのバナーをクリックし、書籍検索してください。書籍詳細ページに音声ダウンロードアイコンがございますのでそちらから自習用音声としてご活用ください。

https://www.seibido.co.jp

Preface

Listen Up, Talk Back is a comprehensive listening and speaking course for elementary to intermediate students. This two-book series has been specially written for Japanese college and university students. The topics in *Listen Up, Talk Back* reflect the kinds of situations students come across both when studying in their home country and abroad. The topics are practical, useful, and generative. Students will be able to use the language they practice in *Listen Up, Talk Back* in everyday situations. Students are introduced to characters whom they will be able to relate to. This approach greatly helps them to tap into existing knowledge, experience, vocabulary, and structures, and to build upon this further.

Each unit focuses on a topic and related vocabulary, functions, and grammar. Students are also provided with a wide range of speaking and listening activities and exercises. These have been carefully written to provide an appropriate amount of support in order to make each task challenging yet achievable.

How to use this book

Warm-up

The warm up activities introduce the topic of the unit. A visual image is provided to help establish the context. Students are invited to draw on and discuss their own experience of the topic. Key vocabulary for the unit is presented to allow for maximum comprehension of the listening tasks.

Listening activities

Listening is a key aspect of this series. Each unit provides three separate listening tasks. Each listening task consists of two to three activities. The listening activities initially focus on general understanding, followed by listening for details. General understanding activities may be to identify who is speaking or to identify the general topic of a conversation. Listening for detail activities include listening for numbers, completing tables with key information, and underlining the correct word in a sentence. Each activity is carefully designed to involve minimal responses as far as possible in order to allow students to focus on listening more than writing.

A wide variety of exercise types is used to maximize student engagement. In addition, students are exposed to a variety of listening texts such as conversations, advertisements, voicemail messages, and announcements. It is advised that teachers allow students to listen to each text a number of times. Students will need repetition of the listening texts in order to focus on the different demands of each activity.

Tips for Communication

These useful, practical tips for everyday communication support the following speaking activities. The tips are drawn from the conversations in the listening exercises, so students get a good sense of the context they relate to. The tips focus on things such as answering the phone, using idioms, addressing people formally and informally, and strategies for keeping a conversation going.

Speaking activities

Speaking practice is an important feature of this series. Each unit offers three opportunities for students to speak within the given topic area. Pair work is a key activity.

In *Talk with a Partner*, students practice simple spoken interactions based on a "chunk" of language they have heard in the Listening texts.

In *Develop Your Speaking Skills*, students first read a scripted dialog aloud, and then introduce different elements to create their own conversation, communicating more freely within the language structures they have encountered. If appropriate, teachers could invite pairs to "perform" their conversations to the rest of the class.

Each of the above exercise types is accompanied by a language box that sets out key vocabulary, expression, and patterns.

In the third speaking activity of each unit, students practice in a range of communication channels, including voicemail messages, advertisements, and announcements. In some units, the third speaking activity gives students guidance to enable them to prepare and give a short talk or a more formal speech. Teachers should give students ample time and support as they prepare their talks or speeches. Encouragement and support is vital to making students feel comfortable about speaking in front of others.

Grammar Focus

In each unit, one element of grammar is highlighted and explained. The grammar point is drawn from the conversations in the listening exercises. A clear explanation is given, with examples. The students complete exercises to consolidate their understanding of the grammar point.

はじめに

本書 *Listen Up, Talk Back* は初中級者向けリスニング・スピーキング力養成のためのテキストとして執筆されました。2つのシリーズ本から構成される本書は、特に日本人大学生を対象に構成されています。トピックは日本人大学生が国内と国外の両方で経験する英会話の場面を、実践的に、有用に、そして発展可能に設定しています。テキストで学んだ表現はそのまま英会話で使用できます。テキストの登場人物は、周りの人たちとの会話のやり取りを繰り広げます。この状況から学ぶことで、英会話で実際に使用される語句、表現、文構造、知識、経験などを疑似体験し、さらなるリスニング・スピーキング技能の向上を望むことができます。

このテキストの各課にて、1つのトピックについて関連する語句・機能・文法を取り上げます。コミュニケーション能力を伸ばすための豊富なヒントとともに、様々なスピーキングとリスニングのタスクを提供しています。

本書ははじめに英語母語話者 James Bean 氏と Gillian Flaherty 氏が原稿を作成し、その内容を日本人英語教員である鎌倉が再構成しています。よって、英語が話される国で使用される自然な表現が、日本人学習者に適切な難易度と情報量になるよう配慮されています。母語話者と非母語話者の協力によって、日本で学ぶ日本人英語学習者が実際の英会話の場で活躍できる力を養える教科書となっています。

最後になりますが、本書の出版の機会を頂いた成美堂社長佐野英一郎氏、御協力を頂いた編集部の佐野泰孝氏、萩原美奈子氏、工藤隆志氏、宍戸貢氏には大変お世話になりました。心からの感謝を申し上げます。

鎌倉　義士

本書の使い方

Warm-up

　各課冒頭にあるWarm-upでは、その課で学ぶトピックに関連する単語を確認します。テキストにあるイラストや画像から語を連想できるよう構成しています。学生の経験を引き出し、その後の会話練習につながるように関連する重要語句をここで学びます。

Listening

　本書の中心となるリスニングは3つもしくは4つから構成されています。各課前半のListening 1と2では日本人学生タカシやヨーコが英語で会話するダイアログを聞き取り、その理解度をテキスト内の設問で測ります。リスニングの内容は会話全体の理解から細部までの理解へと段階的に構成されています。話者は誰か、会話のトピックは何かなど全体的な理解から、数字の聞き取り、表の作成、正しい情報の選択など会話の詳細の理解までを本書で学習できます。内容確認の設問は必要最小限の回答に抑え、学生がリスニングに集中できるよう配慮しています。学生が多種多様な英語による聞き取りを学ぶため、後半のListening 3と4では一人の話者によるモノローグや広告、留守電メッセージ、告知のアナウンスなどを課題としています。英語による実生活で経験する音声を繰り返し聞くことで、学生の幅広いリスニング力を養います。

Tips for Communication

　リスニングの会話内で使用されている英会話でのコツや秘訣を、英語ネイティブ話者の視点から説明しています。その内容はフォーマルから親しげな会話の方法、会話を続けるためのコツ、電話での応対、イディオム・慣用句の使用まで多岐にわたります。英会話を潤滑に行うためのヒントを学生と共有してください。

Talk with a Partner

　スピーキングは本書のもう一つの重要課題です。各課のトピックに関連する3つの会話練習を用意し、ペアワークを中心に展開します。chunkやset phraseと呼ばれるある程度の定形表現を使用しながら、学生が英会話を実践します。

Language Box

　高頻度の定形語句や表現を使用することで、自然に会話が成立するよう構成してあります。

Develop Your Speaking Skills

　Aパートにて学生はテキストのダイアログを読み、その会話を模倣することで会話の流れや、やり取りの方法を学びます。続くBパートにてLanguage Boxの表現を参考に取り入れ、学生が話したい内容をオリジナルの英会話として自由に表現できるよう段階的に練習します。

Speaking

　各課後半のListeningで聞いたモノローグを練習します。会話以外の英語の表現方法を学ぶことで、多種多様な英語表現を聞き取る力を育むことを目的とします。

Grammar Focus

　英会話に役立つ文法知識の確認をドリル練習の問題と共に提供しております。中学・高校で学んだ英文法の確認だけにならぬよう、英会話でどのように使用されているのかの点に注目し、例文とともに説明します。

CONTENTS

Meeting New People

Warm-up

A good way to meet new people and make friends is to join a club. Imagine you are starting at a new university and you want to meet some new people. Look at the list of clubs. Would you like to join any of them?

A Think of other clubs that you might find at a university. Write them in the spaces below.

Social and cultural groups	Sporting groups
Drama Club	Badminton Club
University Choir	Tennis Club
Chess Club	Swimming Club
_____	_____
_____	_____
_____	_____

B Write the correct word from the box beside each meaning.

roommate   introduce   volunteer   online

to tell someone what your name is: _____

a person who works without being paid, just to help others: _____

a person (not family) who lives in the same residence as you: _____

on the Internet: _____

Meet Takashi! He is 20 years old and he comes from Japan. Takashi is studying at a university in the United States, and now he is living in a shared residence with other students.

Listening 1 · 1-02

A Listen to Takashi talking to his new roommate, Jess. Write short answers.

1. Who starts the conversation? _____
2. Who moved in first? _____
3. What event does Jess mention to Takashi? _____
4. What is the last question Takashi asks Jess? _____

B Listen again and check **Takashi** or **Jess**.

	Takashi	Jess
1. Who moved in today?	☐	☐
2. Who decided to stay longer?	☐	☐
3. Who is going to the barbecue?	☐	☐

Tips for Communication

Being friendly

When you meet someone new, it's usual to ask questions. Don't ask anything too personal, though. In Jess and Takashi's conversation, the questions are quite general. They both feel comfortable answering each other's questions. Avoid topics such as girlfriends/boyfriends, religion, and politics.

Sounding friendly

Using a friendly voice is important when talking to someone you haven't met before. It helps to make you both feel relaxed and makes the conversation run smoothly. If you use a friendly voice, it also allows you to ask the other person questions. They won't feel that you are being intrusive and will be more likely to answer your questions, and ask you some, too.

Using a friendly voice is easy. You just need to use the "music" in your voice. Try to make your voice sound interesting by using higher and lower intonation. Avoid speaking with a flat voice. Listen to how people talk in movies or on television. Also, if you smile when you are talking, your voice actually sounds friendlier. Try recording yourself so you can hear what you sound like.

Listening 2

 1-03

A 🎧 Who likes to do these things in their free time? Listen and check **Jess** or **Takashi**.

	Jess	Takashi
1. play basketball	☐	☐
2. play online games	☐	☐
3. eat out	☐	☐
4. go to the gym	☐	☐
5. go to the movies	☐	☐

B 🎧 Who do they do each activity with? Listen again and circle the correct words or names.

1. play basketball with **Jemma** / **friends**
2. study with **roommates** / **Jemma**
3. play online games with **Matt** / **Andy**
4. go to the gym **with friends** / **by myself**

Talk with a Partner

👥 Work with a partner. Take turns to ask: *What do you like to do in your free time?* Use expressions from the box in your answers.

LANGUAGE BOX		
Expressions:	**Example activities:**	**People:**
I often ... with ...	go shopping	friends
I sometimes ... with ...	play soccer	family
I ... with ... twice a week	go to the swimming pool	roommates
We sometimes ...	go to a restaurant	

Grammar Focus

Gerunds

In the first dialog between Jess and Takashi, Jess asks *Do you like swimming?*

In that sentence, *swimming* is a gerund. A gerund is the *-ing* form of a verb used as a noun (for example, *walking, dancing, running, playing*).

Walking is a good way to exercise.

To talk about activities we do in our free time, we can use a verb such as *enjoy*, *like*, or *love* with a gerund.

I love skiing. I enjoy cooking. Do you like playing online games?

Complete the sentences using verbs from the box in the gerund form.

smoke dance listen read shop

1. _____ is bad for your health.
2. _____ is fun and it's a good form of exercise.
3. Rob likes _____ manga comics.
4. Bree loves _____ for clothes.
5. I enjoy _____ to many kinds of music.

Develop Your Speaking Skills

A **You are going to practice introducing yourself. Work in pairs and practice the dialog.**

Kim: Hi. We haven't met. My name is **Kim**.
Takashi: Hello, **Kim**. I'm **Takashi**.
Kim: Nice to meet you, **Takashi**.
Takashi: Nice to meet you, too.
Kim: Where are you from?
Takashi: I'm from **Japan**. How about you?
Kim: I'm from **Denver**.
Takashi: Where is **Denver**?
Kim: It's close to **the Rocky Mountains**.
Takashi: Do you like **skiing**?
Kim: Yes, I do.

B **Now practice in pairs with different students. For each dialog choose a different name, a place, and an activity you like to do.**

LANGUAGE BOX	
A	**B**
Hi. We haven't met yet. My name is …	Hello. I'm …
Nice to meet you, …	Nice to meet you, too.
Where are you from?	I'm from … How about you?
I'm from … Do you like —ing?	Yes, I do / No. I don't

Listening 3: *Announcement*

 1-04

🎧 It is "Move-in Day" at Takashi's new college. Listen to the announcement and circle the correct words in each sentence.

1. This is a day for new students to **move into their rooms** / **start classes**.
2. The volunteers are wearing **blue** / **orange** T-shirts.
3. The **new students** / **volunteers** will take the boxes and bags to the rooms.
4. The new students need to get their room key and a **map** / **hat**.
5. In the evening, students are invited to a **barbecue** / **movie night**.

Listening 4: *Voicemail*

 1-05

A 🎧 Listen to the voicemail message. Circle the correct answer.

Why is Jim calling Takashi?

a. to ask Takashi where the barbecue is taking place
b. to tell Takashi that he'll be late for the barbecue
c. to ask Takashi if he wants to go to the barbecue

B 🎧 Listen again and circle the correct answers.

1. How many messages does Takashi have?

   a. one
   b. two
   c. three

2. What time does Jim want to meet Takashi?

   a. 6:00 p.m.
   b. 6:15 p.m.
   c. 6:50 p.m.

Speaking: *Leave a Voicemail Message*

Work with a partner. Take turns to practice leaving a voicemail message about going to an event. Use expressions from the box.

LANGUAGE BOX				
Hi, ... It's ... here.	I'm calling about the ... I'm calling to see if you'd like to go ... Are you planning to go to the ...?	movie night. barbecue. party. concert.	It starts at ... It's being held ... We could meet at ...	Let me know. You have my number. Bye. Talk to you later.

Warm-up

People live in different kinds of homes. Some people live in a house and some live in an apartment. Some people have a garden and some have a balcony. Some people have one bathroom and some have two bathrooms.

Match the words to the pictures.

a. bathroom

b. basement

c. study

d. balcony

e. apartment

f. garden

g. kitchen

h. house

Meet Bill! He is a 20-year-old student from California. Bill has moved to a different state to study at a university. Now he's living in a shared residence with other students.

Listening 1

🎧 1-06

A 🎧 **Listen and circle the correct answers.**

1. Is the living room big or small?   **big / small**
2. How many bathrooms are there?   **one / two**
3. Where is the clothes dryer?   **in the basement / in the kitchen**

B 🎧 **The house has three levels. Where can you find these items in the house? Listen again and match the levels to the items.**

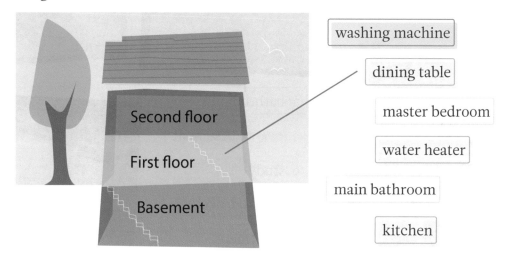

washing machine

dining table

master bedroom

water heater

main bathroom

kitchen

Second floor

First floor

Basement

Tips for Communication

Open questions and closed questions

Jenny asks Bill different kinds of questions.
Does your house have just one bathroom? We call this a **closed question**, because it has only two possible answers, *Yes or No*.

What is your house in California like? This is called an **open question**. Bill can answer it any way he likes. He tells her a lot about his home.

A good way to keep a conversation going is to use lots of open questions. That way, you won't just get a *Yes or No* answer! Here are some examples:
How do you feel about ...? What do you think of ...? What kind of ...?

Listening 2

1-07

A 🎧 Listen to Bill and Laura. Circle the correct answer for each question.

1. What are Bill and Laura talking about?
   a. where they want to live
   b. where they live now
   c. their homes

2. What kind of place do they both live in?
   a. a shared apartment
   b. at home with parents
   c. a dorm

3. What does Laura say she is looking forward to?
   a. moving into a new room
   b. moving into a new dorm
   c. sleeping in her own bed at home

B 🎧 Listen again and check **Bill** or **Laura** for each statement.

	Bill	Laura
1. lives in Shipley	☐	☐
2. has a small room	☐	☐
3. has a view of the sports fields	☐	☐
4. has a view of the parking lot	☐	☐

Talk with a Partner

👥 What is your room like? Talk about your room with a partner. Use expressions from the box.

LANGUAGE BOX		
Question	**Answer**	
What is your room like?	It's ...	comfortable
	It's nice and ...	bright
	I have a great view.	bed
	I can see ...	window
	I like my room.	door
	I have a ... in front of ...	balcony

Grammar Focus

Comparatives

In the dialog between Bill and Laura, Bill says *My bed at home is much more comfortable than my bed here.* Bill uses comparatives to make a comparison between two things. Look at the table below.

Short adjectives				
old	older		tall	taller
Sometimes we double the last letter.				
big	big<u>g</u>er		hot	hot<u>t</u>er
When the adjective ends in –*y*, we use –*ier* in the comparative.				
happy	happ<u>ier</u>		lazy	laz<u>ier</u>
Some adjectives have comparative forms which are very different.				
bad	worse		good	better
Long adjectives				
peaceful	more peaceful		comfortable	more comfortable

Complete the sentences with adjectives from the box. Use the comparative forms of the adjectives.

easy	heavy	good	interesting

1. Your bag isn't very heavy. My bag is _____.
2. The math exam was quite hard. The English exam was _____.
3. The movie wasn't very interesting. The movie I saw last week was

   _____.

4. My French is quite bad. Eric's is _____.

Develop Your Speaking Skills

Work in pairs and practice the dialog. Then talk about different rooms in your home, using comparatives. Use expressions from the box.

A: Which room is bigger? Your kitchen or your living room?

B: The living room is bigger. But the kitchen is brighter. There's a big window in the kitchen.

LANGUAGE BOX			
Question(A)		**Answer(B)**	
Which room is ...?	bigger, quieter	kitchen	The / My / Our ... is ...
Your ... or your ...?	warmer	living room	
	more comfortable	bathroom	But the ... is ...
	brighter, nicer	dining room	We have ...
		bedroom	There's ...

Listening 3: *Short Talk*

 1-08

A 🎧 You are going to give a short talk about your home. First, listen to the model talk below and fill in the blanks.

Hello, I'm Sam. I'm going to talk to you about my home. I live in an apartment in a small ¹_____ on a quiet street. There are five other apartments in the building. My apartment is on the ²_____ floor. It has a living room, a small ³_____ room, a kitchen, a bathroom, laundry, and two ⁴_____, my parents' room and my room. There's also a ⁵_____.

B Now think about your own home. Is it a house or an apartment? Where is it? What rooms does it have?

Write your own short talk in the box below. You may use the words or phrases in the language box to help you. Then present your short talk in class.

YOUR TALK

LANGUAGE BOX
I live in ... a house / an apartment ... ... in a ... building / street ... on the ... floor It has a ... living / dining room / kitchen / bathroom / bedrooms ... There's also a ... balcony / garden / rooftop area

Warm-up

A Look at this "family tree." It shows the people in the family of a young woman called Meg. Some words are missing. Write the words from the box below in the correct places.

> mother   brother   grandmother   aunt

B Write the correct word from the box beside each meaning.

> pick up   get-together   album   place

1. a book for keeping photos in: _____
2. a party, barbeque or informal meeting: _____
3. an informal word for someone's home: _____
4. to stop at a place so someone can get into your car: _____

Meet Meg! She is 20 years old and she comes from Virginia. Now Meg is attending university and is living in a shared residence with other students. But she lives close to her family.

Listening 1

 1-09

A 🎧 **Listen to Meg speaking to her grandmother on the phone. Answer the questions.**

1. What event are they talking about?
2. What does Meg offer to do for her grandmother?

B 🎧 **Listen again. Circle the correct words.**

1. The person who answers the phone is **Meg** / **Meg's grandmother**.
2. Meg's grandmother says she is **feeling bad** / **not doing too badly**.
3. The family get-together will be at Meg's **grandmother's** / **aunt's** place.
4. They both agree that they **will** / **won't** have a lot to talk about.

Tips for Communication

Speaking on the phone

A good way to answer the phone is to say:
Hello. (Your name) speaking.
Hello. Sam Carter speaking.

If you are the person making the call, you can then say: *Hello. It's (Your name) here.*

Hello. It's Kim Benson here.
(If you know the person well, you don't need to give your family name.)

You can then make some "small talk," for example:
How are you?
I'm well, thanks. How about you?

To introduce the main topic, the caller can say:
I'm calling about ...

To finish the call, both people usually say *Bye.*

1-10

Listening 2

🎧 Listen to the conversation between Meg and her friend. Circle the correct answer.

1. Where are the photos they are looking at?
   a. on Meg's phone
   b. on Jim's phone
   c. in a photo album

2. Who does Jim say that Meg looks like?
   a. her mother
   b. her brother
   c. her grandmother

3. How old is Meg's brother?
   a. fifteen
   b. sixteen
   c. seventeen

4. Who does Meg's Grandma live with?
   a. her husband
   b. Meg's parents
   c. She lives alone.

5. How often does Meg see her Grandma who lives close by?
   a. a few times a week
   b. almost every week
   c. a few times a year

Talk with a Partner

👥 Work with a partner. Take turns to ask "*Do you mind if I* ...?" When you respond, you may either agree or refuse. Use expressions from the box.

LANGUAGE BOX		
A	**B**	
Examples: Do you mind if I look at your photos? Do you mind if I sit here? Do you mind if I join you? Do you mind if I ask a question?	**Examples (agreeing):** Not at all. Go ahead. By all means. Sure.	**Examples(refusing):** Sorry, but ... ... they're private. ... I'd rather you didn't. ... I'd rather be alone. ... I'm waiting for someone. ... we don't really have time.

Grammar Focus

Reflexive pronouns

Jim asks Meg if her grandmother lives by herself. The phrase *by + reflexive pronoun* means alone, with no other people.

I can't move this piano **by myself**. *I need help.*   *Mr. Hodge lives* **by himself**.

Herself is a reflexive pronoun. The reflexive pronouns are:

Singular: *myself, yourself, himself, herself, itself*

Plural: *ourselves, yourselves, themselves*

We use reflexive pronouns when the subject and object of a sentence are the same person or thing.

Complete the sentences using reflexive pronouns from the box.

ourselves   yourself   myself

1. Sometimes I enjoy going to see a movie by _____.
2. Can I sit beside you or do you want to be by _____?
3. We did the job by _____, without any help!

Develop Your Speaking Skills

A **You are going to practice speaking on the phone. Work in pairs and practice the dialog.**

A: Hello. Alex Jones speaking.

B: Hi, Alex. It's Sam here.

A: Sam! How are you?

B: I'm well, thanks. I'm calling about the party on Friday night. Are you coming to Ed's place?

A: Yes, I'm hoping to.

B: Would you like me to pick you up?

A: No, thanks. I'll get there by myself.

B: Okay. Well, I'll see you there.

A: Yes, see you there. Bye.

B **Practice with your own names. Start the phone call, then talk about going to an event. Use expressions from the box.**

LANGUAGE BOX	
B	**A**
I'm calling about ... Are you ...? Would you like me to pick you up? How about I pick you up at ...? / Okay. Well, I'll see you there.	Yes, I'm hoping to. Yes, please. / No, thanks. I'll get there by myself. That sounds perfect. I'll be waiting at ...
Events	
barbeque at Tina's house on Saturday afternoon (starts at 2 p.m.) concert at City Hall on Tuesday evening (starts at 7 p.m.)	

Listening 3: *Advertisement*

A 🎧 **Listen to the radio advertisement and fill in the blanks.**

This **Sunday**, May 9, is **Mother's Day**. Make it a **special day** for the **special woman** in your ¹_____. **Join** us at **Vera's Restaurant** for a **delicious buffet** ²_____.

Vera's Restaurant has a **charming atmosphere**, with **delightful views** over the **Blackwood River**.

Our **buffet menu** offers a **great variety** of ³_____ to choose from, with something for **every member** of **the family**, **young or old**. Prices are **$35** for **adults**, and **$20** for **children 12 years and** ⁴_____.

Vera's Restaurant is ⁵_____ on **Mother's Day** between **11 a.m. and 5 p.m.** Reservations are **essential**, so call **855 565-2270** to be sure of a place. Bring the **whole family** to **Vera's Restaurant** for a **Mother's Day celebration** to ⁶_____!

> What does "buffet" mean? Buffet is a way of serving food in restaurants. Waiters don't bring dishes to people at their tables. Instead, food is laid out in one part of the room, and people go and serve themselves. They take a plate and then choose the food they want to eat.

B Are the sentences true or false? Circle **T** for true or **F** for false.
1. The radio advertisement is played in the days before Mother's Day.   T / F
2. Vera's Restaurant is not far from a river.   T / F
3. Children are not allowed into Vera's Restaurant.   T / F
4. The restaurant is open for dinner in the evening on Mother's Day.   T / F
5. The restaurant will probably be busy on Mother's Day.   T / F

Read the Advertisement Aloud

Now pretend that you are a radio announcer. Read the advertisement for Vera's Restaurant aloud. Include the words that you wrote to fill the blanks. Speak slowly and clearly. Use intonation—stress the important words (make them stronger). Practice by stressing the **bold** words in the radio advertisement above.

You may practice silently to yourself first. Then read the advertisement aloud to a partner or to your class.

Transportation in the City

Warm-up

Imagine that you are visiting a city in another country. It is your first time in this city. You will have to find out where different places are.

A **What are some of the places that you want to visit? Work with a partner and add some more places to the list.**

<u>   train station   </u>   <u>   shopping mall   </u>   <u>   </u>

<u>   </u>   <u>   </u>   <u>   </u>

B **There are many ways to ask where something is. Some are more polite than others. Read the sentences and number them from 1 to 5. 1 is the most polite and 5 is the least polite.**

1. I'm looking for the station. ☐

3. Where is the station? ☐

2. Could you tell me where the station is? ☐

Asking where things are

5. Can you tell me where the station is? ☐

4. Would you be able to tell me where the station is? ☐

17

Meet Yoko! She is 19 years old and she lives in Japan. Yoko is studying at university.

Listening 1 🎧 1-12

A 🎧 Listen to Yoko talking to a tourist. Circle **T** for true or **F** for false for each statement.

1. Yoko talks to the tourist first.   T / F
2. The tourist wants to go to City Park.   T / F
3. Meiji Park is nearby.   T / F
4. Yoko tells the tourist to take a bus.   T / F

B 🎧 Listen again. Check the information that Yoko gives the tourist.

1. how long the bus takes   ☐
2. where to catch the bus   ☐
3. how much the bus costs   ☐
4. how to get back from Meiji Park   ☐

Tips for Communication

Using *No problem*

No problem is a very useful expression. You can use it after someone says, "*Thank you.*" for something. It means that you were happy to help. It is often a good way to end a conversation. Yoko uses *no problem* at the end of the conversation:

Thanks for all of your help.

No problem.

Listening 2

🎧 1-13

🎧 Listen to Yoko talking to a tourist. Circle the correct words in each sentence.

1. The man wants to go to Aozora **Road** / **Mall**.
2. Yoko says it will take about **ten** / **five** minutes to walk there.
3. Yoko tells the man to turn **right** / **left** into Reiwa Street.
4. The mall is on the **left** / **right** side of the street.
5. The man can take the number **324** / **342** bus back.

Talk with a Partner

Work with a partner. Use the map. Take turns to ask for directions to a location on the map. Use expressions from the box in your answers.

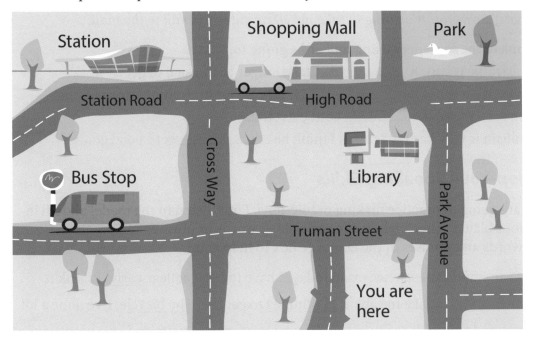

LANGUAGE BOX	
Asking for directions	**Showing directions**
Excuse me. / I'm looking for ...	It's next to/on/at/in the ...
Can you tell me ...?	It's quite ... / It's not ...
Could you tell me ...?	Take a ...
Would you be able to tell me ...?	It will take ...
Where is ...? / Is there ...?	You'll have to ...
How long ...?	Walk along ... / Turn left into ... / Cross ...
	You'll see it on ...
Thanks for your help.	
Thanks for all of your help.	No problem. / You're welcome.

Grammar Focus

Will and *be going to* for predictions

In the first dialog between Yoko and the tourist, Yoko uses *will* to predict the length of the bus ride to Meiji Park.

It'll take about 20 minutes.

In the second dialog, Yoko uses *will* to predict the length of the walk to Aozora Mall.

It'll take you about ten minutes.

In both examples, she is making a prediction about what will happen in the future. If the prediction is based on some kind of evidence that we can see now, we can use *be going to* instead.

The bus is late. I'm going to be late for work.

I have a sore foot. It's going to take me 20 minutes to walk to the mall.

Complete the sentences using *will* or *be going to*.

1. The traffic is bad. It _____ take longer than usual to get to work.
2. The station is not far. It _____ take about five minutes to walk there.
3. I'm sure Freda _____ be at class today.
4. William is very hard-working. I think he _____ get a good grade.

Develop Your Speaking Skills

 1-14

You are going to practice making predictions. First, listen to the model and fill in the four blanks. Then change the underlined words or phrases and practice. Use the words and phrases in the language box to help you.

I have an important science exam today. I have to be at college <u>early</u>. I think it

¹_____ take me about <u>15 minutes</u> to get there <u>by bicycle</u>. I've done a lot

of work so I think I ²_____ get a good grade. My friend, Joe hasn't done

enough work. I think he ³_____ find the exam difficult. I think we

⁴_____ both be very happy when the exam is over.

LANGUAGE BOX		
Arrive at	**Travel time**	**Travel method**
at 8 o'clock	20 minutes	by foot
earlier than usual	half an hour	by bus
at lunch time	ten minutes	by train

Listening 3: Announcement   1-15

A 🎧 Yoko is waiting for a train. Listen to the announcement and circle the words you hear.

1. The problem will affect **all trains** / **four trains**.

2. The problem was caused by **a damaged train** / **the heavy rain**.

3. They hope to deal with the problem **after 8:30** / **before 8:30**.

B 🎧 Now listen again and complete the notice.

> THE FOLLOWING TRAINS TO THE CITY WILL BE DELAYED:
> ¹_____, 8:00, 8:15 and ²_____
> These trains will be ³_____ minutes late.
> We ⁴_____ for the inconvenience.
> Please go to the ⁵_____ _____ if you need any further help.

Listening 4: Short Talk   1-16

A 🎧 You are going to give a talk about how to get from your house to a nearby place. First, listen to the model talk below and fill in the blanks.

The ¹_____ is not far from my house. I can walk there easily. It takes me about ²_____ minutes. First, I walk along my street and turn ³_____ onto Senbon Street. Then, I ⁴_____ Senbon Street and I turn left onto Gojo Street. I walk along Gojo Street and turn ⁵_____ onto Karasuma Street. The station is on the ⁶_____.

B Now think about a place that you can walk to from your house. It may be a station, bus stop, mall, store, park, or any other place. Think about how to get to this place from your home.

Write your own short talk in the box below. You may use the words or phrases in the language box to help you.

> **YOUR TALK**
>
>
>
>
>
>

> **LANGUAGE BOX**
> ... is not far from my house / I can ... there ... / It takes me about ...
> First, I walk ... and turn ... / Then, I ... / The ... is ...

Shopping

Warm-up

Do you know the different sections in a supermarket?

A **Where would you find these products? Write them in their correct sections.**

> bacon / cakes / corn flakes / garbage bags / ice cream / toothpaste /
> yogurt / orange juice

BAKERY

1. _____

BREAKFAST CEREAL

2. _____

DAIRY

3. _____

DENTAL CARE

4. _____

FROZEN FOODS

5. _____

HOUSEHOLD ITEMS

6. _____

MEAT

7. _____

BEVERAGES AND DRINKS

8. _____

B **Match the words and meanings.**

1. aisle • • **a.** one part of a supermarket or big store
2. brand • • **b.** a person who sells things and helps customers in a store
3. clerk • • **c.** the food and other things you need to buy for your home
4. groceries • • **d.** a type of product made by a company, with its own name
5. section • • **e.** the group of people who work in a store, company or office
6. staff • • **f.** the long space where you walk between shelves in a supermarket or big store

Listening 1

 1-17

A 🎧 Takashi is in a supermarket. Listen to him asking a clerk for help. Answer the questions.

1. What does Takashi want to know?

   a. where certain products are   **b.** the price of certain products

2. How many different products does Takashi ask about?

   a. two   **b.** three

3. What does the clerk ask Takashi to explain?

   a. what edamame taste like   **b.** what edamame are

B 🎧 Listen again. Circle the correct words.

1. The Frozen Foods section is in **Aisle 5** / **Aisle 9**.

2. Takashi wants to buy **a toothbrush** / **some toothpaste**.

3. The clerk sends Takashi to the **Dental Care** / **Health and Hair** section.

Tips for Communication

Asking for help
A simple, polite way to ask for help in a store is to say: *Excuse me, can you help me?* Here are some other expressions:
I wonder if you can help me. *I'm looking for …* *Do you have any …?* *I need …* *Where will I find …?*
It's nice to thank someone after they help you.
Thanks for your help. *Thank you. You've been very helpful.*

Listening 2

 1-18

A What are the prices for the bottles of sunscreen? Listen and write the prices.

Small: $9.95

Large: $＿＿＿＿＿＿＿

Small: $＿＿＿＿＿＿＿

Large: $＿＿＿＿＿＿＿

B 🎧 Listen again and complete the following sentences.

1. How ＿＿＿＿＿＿＿ is this bottle of Pro-Tec sunscreen?

2. Does it come in a ＿＿＿＿＿＿＿ size?

3. Is there a cheaper ＿＿＿＿＿＿＿?

Talk with a Partner

👥 Work with a partner. Take turns to ask and answer. Use expressions from the box.

LANGUAGE BOX	
Customer	**Clerk**
Excuse me, can you help me?	Sure. How can I help?
I'm looking for ... frozen vegetables / toothpaste / yogurt And where's that?	It's in ... / They're in ... Frozen Foods / Dental Care / Dairy section Aisle 2 / Aisle 5
Thanks for your help.	You're welcome.

Grammar Focus

How much? How many?

Takashi asks about prices using questions with *How much …?*

How much is this bottle of Pro-Tec sunscreen? How much is that?

We use *How much …? / How many …?* to ask about amounts or numbers.

How many … is for countable nouns, such as people, years, and apples.

How much … is for uncountable nouns, such as money, water, and time.

COUNTABLE NOUNS: *How many …?*	UNCOUNTABLE NOUNS: *How much …?*
How many people are coming?	*How much money shall I bring?*
How many years has he lived here?	*How much water do you want?*
How many apples shall I buy?	*How much time do we have left?*

Complete the questions using much or many, then match to the answers.

Questions | Answers
| | |

1. How _____ rice do we have? • • Two – a boy and a girl.
2. How _____ cars are in the parking lot? • • None. I'll go and buy some.
3. How _____ children do you have? • • $22.
4. How _____ do you make per hour? • • Just a few – maybe 15 or 20.

Develop Your Speaking Skills

A You are going to ask about prices. Work in pairs and practice the dialog.

Customer: Excuse me, how much is this bottle of Kof-Go cough syrup?
Clerk: That's $11.99.
Customer: Is there a cheaper brand?
Clerk: Yes, Di-Tuss cough syrup is cheaper. It's $9.99 a bottle.
Customer: I'll take a bottle of Di-Tuss, please.

B Now practice. Customer: first ask about the product in Column A. Then ask for a cheaper brand. Clerk: tell the customer about the prices. The cheaper brand is in Column B. Use expressions from the box.

Products	A	B
bottle of mouthwash	Freshness $8.95	Clean Breath $6.99
tube of toothpaste	Glisten $4.90	Oral Care $3.50

LANGUAGE BOX	
Customer	**Clerk**
Excuse me, how much is this …	That's …
Is there a cheaper brand?	Yes, … It's …
I'll take …, please.	Sure. Is there anything else I can help you with?
No, that's all, thanks.	

Listening 3: Short Talk

A 🎧 **You are going to give a short talk about a store. First, listen to the model talk below and fill in the blanks.**

Hello, I'm Taka. I'm going to talk to you about a store where I like to

¹_____.

Near my house, there is a small grocery store. I buy my groceries there. It's not

as ²_____ as the supermarket, but it's ³_____ to my house.

I can get most of the ⁴_____ that I need there. The staff at the corner

store are ⁵_____ and helpful.

B **Now think about a store where you like to shop. It may be a grocery store, or any other kind of store. Think about things they sell at this store, the people who work there, and why you like to shop there.**

Write your own short talk in the box below. You may use the words or phrases in the language box to help you. Then present your own short talk in class.

YOUR TALK

LANGUAGE BOX
in my town / near my house / near my apartment / in the city center ... There's a ... book / music / shoe / clothing / grocery ... I buy ... / I get ... I can get ... The staff are ...

UNIT 06 *Celebrations*

Warm-up

We celebrate many different things in life. We celebrate different occasions in different ways.

A How do we celebrate these occasions? Write the letters next to the celebrations. You can use each letter as many times as you like.

Celebration	Ways to celebrate
Wedding _____ Birthday _____ Graduation _____	a. Everyone wears nice clothes. b. There is a party. c. There is a special ceremony. d. There is a cake and presents. e. People walk onto a stage.

B Write the correct word from the box beside each meaning.

1. to do something special to acknowledge a happy event: _____
2. to make somewhere look nice by adding nice things: _____
3. a formal event to celebrate a special occasion: _____
4. a place where you can hold a celebration: _____

ceremony   celebrate   decorate   venue

Listening 1

A 🎧 **Listen to Bill talking to Julia. Circle the correct words.**

1. Bill is organizing a **party** / **dinner** at a restaurant.
2. The celebration is for a **graduation** / **birthday**.
3. Julia **asks Bill for help** / **offers to help Bill**.
4. Bill and Julia talk about **whether they need food** / **what kind of food to have**.
5. Julia says she will **decorate** / **book** the venue.

B 🎧 **Listen again. Write short answers to the questions.**

1. Who is the party for?   _____
2. What kind of food does Julia suggest?   _____
3. What kind of food does Bill suggest?   _____
4. When is the party?   _____

Tips for Communication

Making suggestions

There are different ways to make suggestions. When Bill and Julia are talking about what food to have at the party, Julia says: **How about** pizza?

Bill says: *Oh, Emma's not crazy about pizza.* **Why don't we** *order Thai food? She loves Thai food.*

Bill gives a reason for not ordering pizza. Then he gives a different suggestion.

Here are some more examples following the same pattern:

A: *How about going to the movies tonight?*
B: *I went to the movies last night. Why don't we go out for dinner? We haven't been out for dinner for a long time.*

A: *I'm looking for a necklace for a friend.*
B: *We have some lovely necklaces. Why don't you have a look at these?*

Listening 2

 1-21

A 🎧 **Listen to Bill talking to an assistant in a store. Circle the correct answer.**

1. What occasion is Bill buying a present for?
   a. a wedding   **b.** a graduation   **c.** a birthday

2. Where was the necklace made?
   a. India   **b.** Indonesia   **c.** Indiana

3. How much does the necklace cost?
   a. 45 dollars   **b.** 55 dollars   **c.** 65 dollars

4. What does the store assistant get for Bill?
   a. a receipt   **b.** a box   **c.** a bag

B 🎧 **Listen again. Complete the sentences as you listen.**

1. I'm looking for a _____ for a friend.
2. Can I have a look at this _____, round one?
3. What's it _____ of?
4. Do you know where it was _____?

Talk with a Partner

Work with a partner. Use the pictures. Take turns to ask for information about each item. Use expressions from the box in your questions and answers.

LANGUAGE BOX	
Giving information	**Asking for information**
Can I help you?	I'm looking for ...
No problem.	Can I have a look at ...?
We have some lovely ...	What's it made of?
Why don't you have a look at ...?	Do you know where it was made?
Here you are.	How much is it?
It's made of silver / gold / copper.	I'll take it.
It was made in Thailand / Mexico / India.	
It's ... dollars.	

Grammar Focus

Present perfect tense and *for* and *since*

In his speech, Bill uses the present perfect form.

Emma and I have been friends for nearly six years.

This means that their friendship started nearly six years ago, and continues today. We use present perfect tense to talk about a period of time that started in the past and continues until now.

We form the present perfect using *have / has + past participle*.

Here are some more examples:

I **have known** Dave **since** I was five years old.

I **have lived** here **for** three years.

I **haven't been** to France but I **have been** to Italy.

We use *for* with a period of time: *for the past two days / for three years*

We use *since* with a point in time: *since nine o'clock / since February*

We can use present perfect to ask questions:

Have you known Gina for a long time?   *No, I haven't. / Yes, I have.*

Have you been to China?   *No, I haven't. / Yes, I have.*

A Write the questions using present prefect tense.

1. you / be / the USA?   *Have you been to the USA?*

2. you / read / *Oliver Twist* by Charles Dickens? _____

3. you / live / in another country?   _____

4. you / meet / anyone famous?   _____

B Now write your answers to the questions.

1. _____   3. _____

2. _____   4. _____

Develop Your Speaking Skills

You are going to practice asking and answering questions using present perfect. Take turns with a partner to ask and answer the questions. Use the topics in the box below.

Places	Books	Experiences
• China • Thailand • the UK • France	• *Peter Pan* by JM Barrie • *The Hunger Games* by Suzanne Collins • *Harry Potter* by JK Rowling	• try Indian food • change your hair color • drive a car • travel by plane

Listening 3: *Speech*

 1-22

🎧 **Bill makes a speech at his friend Emma's birthday party. Listen and fill in the blanks.**

Can I have your attention? I just want to say a ¹_____ words. We are all here to ²_____ Emma's birthday.

<u>Emma</u> and I have been friends for ³_____ <u>six years</u>. <u>She</u>'s a <u>fantastic</u> person and a great friend. <u>She</u>'s kind, <u>smart</u> and funny.

Whenever I have a ⁴_____, <u>Emma</u> is the first person I go to. <u>She</u> ⁵_____ gives me good advice.

So, thank you for coming to <u>Emma's</u> birthday party. I hope you're all ⁶_____ yourselves!

Speaking

Now it is your turn. Change the underlined words and write your own birthday speech for a friend's birthday. Use the words and phrases in the language box to help you.

YOUR TALK

LANGUAGE BOX

six months / one year / three years ...
She's a wonderful / fabulous / great person ...
She's clever / helpful / generous / caring ...

DONATIONS

VOLUNTE

Warm-up

Volunteering means working to help others without being paid. Do you volunteer? If not, have you thought about volunteering?

A **Look at the pictures of people volunteering. Match the volunteer jobs to the pictures. Write the numbers of the pictures.**

a. being a tour guide _____

b. helping children learn to read _____

c. providing clothes to the people in need _____

d. picking up litter in streets and parks _____

e. helping children get to and from school safely _____

B **Now look at what some people say about why they volunteer. Which volunteer jobs do you think would suit them? Discuss your ideas with a partner.**

"I love kids."   "I love meeting new people."   "I believe it's good to help people."

"I want to improve my skills and knowledge."

"I want to make my neighborhood a better place."

Listening 1

 1-23

🎧 Yoko is a volunteer tour guide. Listen to her speaking with Mr. and Mrs. Downer. Circle the correct words.

1. Yoko **has** / **has not** met these people before.
2. The Downers want Yoko to call them by their **first names** / **family names**.
3. The Downers **have** / **have not** visited Japan before.
4. The weather is **fine** / **rainy**.
5. They will see the city sights **on foot** / **by bus**.
6. Angela is interested in seeing the **fish market** / **cherry blossoms**.

Tips for Communication

First name or family name?

Yoko begins by calling the visitors Mr. and Mrs. Downer, but they want her to use their first names. Mr. Downer says: *I'm Brian.* Mrs. Downer says: *Please call me Angela.*

Whether you address someone by their first name depends on your relationship with them and how formal you wish to be.

In informal and social situations, first names are suitable:
You're Jean, aren't you? I'm Kim.   Hi, Kim. Nice to meet you.

To ask someone if it's okay to call them by your first name, you can say:
Do you mind if I call you ... ?
To ask people to call you by your first name, you can say:
Please call me ....

Listening 2

 1-24

🎧 Listen to the phone conversation between Yoko and Brian. Circle the correct answer.

1. What time of day is it?
   a. morning
   b. afternoon
   c. evening

2. What did the Downers do when they got back to their hotel after the tour?
   a. They relaxed.
   b. They went out for a meal.
   c. They met some other travelers.

3. Where will they go tonight?
   a. to a traditional restaurant
   b. to a traditional theater
   c. to another hotel

4. What time will Yoko come to their hotel?
   a. 6:00 p.m.
   b. 6:30 p.m.
   c. 7:00 p.m.

Talk with a Partner

👥 Work with a partner. Take turns to ask and answer. Use expressions from the box.

LANGUAGE BOX	
A	**B**
What time is our booking at the restaurant?	Six / Seven / Eight o'clock.
That sounds good. Who else will be joining us?	How about I come to your hotel at ...?
See you at ...	There'll be some other visitors, from China / Australia / France ...

Grammar Focus

The conjunction *so*

Yoko says: It *may get a little cold this evening, so please bring your jackets.*

So is a conjunction, a word joining two sentences into one.

The second sentence follows as a result of the first sentence: It may be cold. As a result, Yoko tells the Downers to bring jackets.

We can use *so* to give a reason when we give advice.

Here are some more examples:

FIRST SENTENCE (reason)		SECOND SENTENCE (advice)
It will probably rain,	so	bring an umbrella.
This road is very busy,	so	take care when you cross it.
You have lots of work to do,	so	get started now!

Match the pairs of sentences. Then say the complete sentences aloud, with *so* between the two parts.

1. The sidewalk is wet. • • Don't be late.
2. You look very tired. • • Lock your car.
3. We all want to leave on time. • • Walk carefully and don't run!
4. Sometimes things get stolen here. • • Stop and take a break.

Develop Your Speaking Skills

A You are going to practice introducing yourself to visitors from other countries. Work in pairs and practice the dialog.

A: Good morning. Are you Mr. West?
B: Yes, I am. Are you the tour guide?
A: Yes, I am. My name is [...], and I'll be your tour guide for this morning.
B: Nice to meet you.
A: Nice to meet you, Mr. West.

B: Please call me Mike.
A: Where are you from, Mike?
B: I'm from Boston in the United States.
A: Welcome to Japan! Is this your first visit here?
B: Yes, it is.
A: Well, we have a lot to see, so let's get started!

B Now practice with different names and countries. Use expressions from the box.

LANGUAGE BOX	
A	**B**
Good morning. Are you Mr. / Ms. ...? Yes, I am. My name is ..., and I'll be ... Nice to meet you, Mr./Ms. ... Where are you from? Welcome to Japan! Is this your first visit here? Well, we have a lot to see, so let's get started!	Yes, I am. Are you the tour guide? Nice to meet you. Please call me ... I'm from ... Yes, it is. / No, I've been here before.

Men's names (Mr.)	Women's names (Ms.)	Cities and countries
Jeff Taylor Tom Harris	Sue Walker Lisa Martin	Sydney, Australia Toronto, Canada

Listening 3: *Announcement*

 1-25

A 🎧 The president of Friends of Fernwood Park is speaking to a group of volunteers. Listen and fill in the blanks.

Good morning, everyone. My name is **Jeff Dean** and I'm the **president** of **Friends of Fernwood Park**. **Thank you** for coming to **join** us for our **clean-up morning**. As you may know, we **meet** on the **first Sunday** of **every month** to **pick up**

¹_____ here in the **park**.

Our **volunteer coordinators**, **Mark and Linda**, will give you **large plastic**

²_____ to put **litter** in.

You were all asked to **bring** your own ³_____, but if you **haven't**

brought a pair, we have some **spare pairs** here.

And we have **plenty of** ⁴_____ here for you to **drink** if you get **thirsty**.

Well, it's time to **get started**. We'll be here for **four hours**, until **one o'clock**. We **love Fernwood Park** and we **love taking care** of it. We couldn't do it **without the help** of wonderful ⁵_____ like you, so **once again**, **thanks** for coming to **help** today.

B 🎧 Listen again. Are the sentences true or false? Circle **T** for true or **F** for false.
1. Friends of Fernwood Park has a clean-up morning once a week. T / F
2. Friends of Fernwood Park has some pairs of gloves for people to wear. T / F
3. The volunteers will be watering the plants in the park. T / F
4. The volunteers will be working all through the day. T / F

Read the Announcement Aloud

Now pretend that you are the president of Friends of Fernwood Park. Read the announcement aloud. Include the words that you wrote to fill the blanks.

Speak slowly and clearly. Use intonation—stress the important words (make them stronger). Practice by stressing the **bold** words in the announcement above.

You may practice silently to yourself first. Then read the announcement aloud to a partner or to your class.

Warm-up

A There are different things we can do to stay well. Write *H* for healthy or *U* for unhealthy next to each habit. Then compare your answers with a partner.

1. Sarah eats lots of fresh fruit and vegetables. _____

2. Tim doesn't have breakfast every day. _____

3. Laura goes to bed late every night. _____

4. Andy goes to the gym three times a week. _____

B Read the sentences. Write the meaning of each underlined word. Choose from the box.

> to help someone to do something by giving support / often / unhealthy food that is quick and easy to eat / not allowed to exist / the way you live your life

1. We shouldn't eat too much junk food. _____

2. Some people believe that soda should be banned. _____

3. We should encourage people to be healthy. _____

4. We should all try to have a healthy lifestyle. _____

5. Kim is fit and healthy. She exercises regularly. _____

37

Listening 1

 1-26

A 🎧 Listen to Bill talking with Helen. Number the topics from **1** to **4** as you listen.

a. _____ Eating healthy food

b. _____ Getting enough sleep

c. _____ Going to the gym

d. _____ Taking lunch to college

B 🎧 Listen again. Circle the correct words.

1. Helen **feels** / **doesn't feel** very healthy.

2. Bill goes to the gym **two** / **three** times a week.

3. Bill **usually** / **always** takes food to college.

4. Helen **doesn't like** / **would like** to exercise.

Tips for Communication

Describing strategies to achieve a goal

Bill tells Helen about what he does to stay fit and healthy. He talks about what he usually does in order to achieve this goal.

I try to *get to the gym three times a week.*

I try to *eat healthy food and I drink a lot of water.*

I usually *take food to college, so I don't have to have lunch in a café.*

I always make sure *I get enough sleep.*

Here is another example following the same pattern:

A: *We have so much college work to do. How do you manage to keep up?*

B: *I try to go to the library in between classes. I usually do some college work at the weekend. And I always make sure I do a few hours work after dinner each night.*

Listening 2

 1-27

🎧 Listen to Bill talking to Annie. Who has the following opinions? Write **B** for Bill or **A** for Annie or **B**+**A** for both.

1. Junk food should be banned. _____
2. Unhealthy food should be more expensive. _____
3. We should encourage people to eat healthily and exercise. _____
4. Schools should do more to educate children about health. _____

Talk with a Partner

Work with a partner. Take turns to give an opinion about staying fit and healthy. The other person should agree with the opinion and add another relevant point. Use expressions from the box in your questions and answers.

LANGUAGE BOX

Opinion
• I think people should exercise three times a week.
• I think schools should do more to educate children about health.
• I think junk food should be banned.

Agreeing with an opinion	Adding another relevant point
Yes, I totally agree ... I think you're right ... I think so, too ... I agree with you ...	And ... I also think that ...

Grammar Focus

Passive voice

Bill uses the passive voice when they are talking about their opinion about junk food.

*I think it should **be banned**.*

In this sentence, Bill uses passive voice because he is not focusing on who should ban junk food. He is focusing on his opinion that it should be banned.

Compare with the following sentence:

***The government** should **ban** junk food.*

In this active sentence, it is clear who should ban junk food. It is the focus of the sentence.

Here are some more examples:

*Unhealthy food should **be banned**.*

*Healthy food should **be made** cheaper.*

*Eating well should **be encouraged**.*

*The amount of sport at school should **be increased**.*

Complete the sentences in passive voice or active voice. Use the verbs in the box.

ban play increase educate make

1. Unhealthy food should _____ more expensive.
2. Children should _____ more sport.
3. Sweet drinks should _____.
4. Everyone should _____ about how to be healthy.
5. The government should _____ the price of junk food.

Develop Your Speaking Skills

You are going to practice talking about opinions using passive voice. Take turns with a partner to present an opinion. Use the topics, verbs and reasons in the table below.

Topics	Verbs	Reasons
junk food soda healthy food and regular exercise unhealthy food doing sport at school	ban encourage increase make	because it's got too much sugar. because it's so bad for your health. because it's the best way to improve your health. because they are more likely to become healthy adults.

Listening 3: *Short Talk*

🎧 1-28

🎧 **You are going to give a short talk about staying fit and healthy. First, listen to the model talk below and fill in the blanks.**

Hello, I'm Bill. I'm talking about staying fit and healthy today. Staying fit and healthy is important to me. These are some of the things I do to stay fit and ¹_____. I make sure I get ²_____ sleep. I think that's ³_____. And I try to eat ⁴_____ food. I don't eat junk food and I drink a lot of water. I also ⁵_____ regularly. I try to get to the gym three times a week. I also play ⁶_____ on the weekends.

Speaking

Now think about what you do to stay fit and healthy. Write your own short talk in the box below. You may use the words or phrases in the language box to help you.

YOUR TALK

LANGUAGE BOX
I try to ... I make sure I ... healthy food ... exercise ... go to ... junk food ... drink water ... play ...

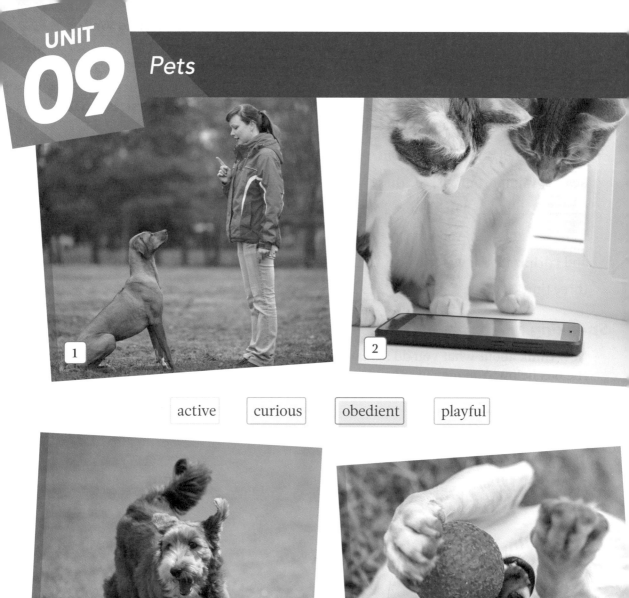

active   curious   obedient   playful

Warm-up

A Look at the pictures of cats and dogs, and look at the list of words that describe their characteristics. Which pictures show the different characteristics? Compare your ideas with a partner.

B Some people prefer dogs and others prefer cats. Which do you prefer?
Are you a "dog person" or a "cat person"? Or are you neither? Talk with a partner.

Listening 1

🎧 1-29

A 🎧 Listen to Meg and Jim talking about their pets. Are the sentences true or false? Circle **T** for true or **F** for false.

1. They are looking at a photo of Meg's pet.   T / F
2. Cleo is the first cat Jim has ever owned.   T / F
3. Meg thinks cats are friendlier than dogs.   T / F
4. Jim's cat sometimes sits on his lap and purrs.   T / F
5. Meg likes walking her dog.   T / F

B 🎧 Listen again. Meg and Jim use various words to describe cats and dogs. Look at the list of words. Write **C** for cat or **D** for dog beside the words as you hear them.

1. elegant _____
2. friendly _____
3. loyal _____
4. calm _____
5. noisy _____

Tips for Communication

Using *I guess*
Jim says: *I guess you could call me a cat person!*

He also says to Meg: *I guess you're more of a dog person, right?*

We use *I guess* in informal conversations to show that we are not very certain or serious about what we are saying. Using *I guess* gives the sense that you want to keep things friendly and light rather than expressing strong opinions.

A: Where's Ben?   B: He's gone out for lunch, I guess. (but I'm not sure)

I guess you're sad that Andy is going away. (but maybe I'm wrong)

In answering a Yes/No question, saying *I guess so* is a way of saying *Yes*, but not very strongly.

A: Are you looking forward to the party tonight?   B: I guess so.

Note that *I guess* is best used in informal conversations. Using it on a more formal situation, such as a job interview or work conversation might make it seem as if you don't care too much about what you are saying. In those situations, it could be better to say, *I believe ...* or *I'd say ...*

Listening 2

 1-30

A 🎧 Listen to Meg speaking with a vet about her dog. Answer the questions.

1. Was Meg able to find out what the problem was herself? _____

2. Is the vet able to fix the problem? _____

B 🎧 Listen again. Circle the correct words.

1. Sandy's front **left** / **right** paw is sore.

2. Dr. Rankin asks Meg to **take a look at the paw** / **hold Sandy**.

3. There is a piece of **wood** / **glass** in Sandy's paw.

4. Dr. Rankin tells Meg to put **some cream** / **a bandage** on the paw.

A *vet* is an animal doctor. (short for "veterinarian")

An animal's *paw* is its foot.

A *limp* is the way you walk if you have a sore foot, with more weight on one foot than the other. Meg's dog is *walking with a limp* because it has a sore paw.

You hold *tweezers* in your fingers and use them pull out sharp things or hairs.

Talk with a Partner

👥 You are going to practice talking about pets. If you have a pet, talk about it. If you don't have one, look at one of the pictures at the start of this unit and imagine you own it. Use expressions from the box.

LANGUAGE BOX

Do you have a pet?

Yes, I have a ...she's / he's called ...

Is this her / him in the photo?

Yes, that's ...

She/He looks like a nice ...

She's/He's very active / curious / obedient / playful ...

I like it when ...

Grammar Focus

The present perfect continuous

Meg says: **He's been walking with a limp** *for the past two days.*

We use the present perfect continuous tense to talk about an action that started at a time in the past and is still happening now.

The structure is: *has/have* + *been* + *-ing* verb form.

We use *for* with a period of time: *for the past two days / for three years*

We use *since* with a point in time: *since nine o'clock / since February*

Here are some more examples:

It has been raining since Friday.   **You have been playing games for** hours!

Put the verbs into the present perfect continuous.

1. I _____ (**try**) to call you for two days!
2. I _____ (**wait**) for the bus since six o'clock.
3. Anna _____ (**learn**) Spanish for five years.
4. John _____ (**feel**) sick since lunchtime.

Develop Your Speaking Skills

A Practice talking to a vet about your pet. Work in pairs.

Vet: Good morning, Kim. Bring your cat in.
Kim: Hello, Dr. Smith. This is Blinky.
Vet: Hello, Blinky. So, what seems to be the problem?
Kim: She's been shaking her head a lot for the past week. I think she may have a sore ear.
Vet: I see. I'll take a look.

B Now practice with these different names and problems.

Vet: Dr. Lee **Owner**: Jo **Pet**: Milo, a cat	**Problem**: He hasn't been eating for two days; breath has been smelling bad; may have a sore tooth
Vet: Dr. Dean **Owner**: Alex **Pet**: Pixie, a dog	**Problem**: She has been vomiting since yesterday; hasn't been eating; may have eaten something bad

LANGUAGE BOX	
Vet	**Owner**
Good morning ... Bring your ... in. What seems to be the problem? I see. I'll take a look.	This is .... She's/He's been ... She/He hasn't been ... I think she/he may ...

09

Listening 3: *Advertisement*

🎧 1-31

A 🎧 Listen to the radio advertisement and fill in the blanks.

Is your **dog** your **best friend**? Then you'll want to give him or her the **best possible** ¹_____. That's where **Bow Wow Pet Services** comes in!

At **Bow Wow**, we've been **taking care of dogs** for over **15 years**. We offer a **range of services**, including ²_____ and **blow-drying**, **clipping and styling**. All of our **groomers** are very **experienced** and know how to keep your **special friend healthy** and ³_____. We are all **dog owners** ourselves!

If you're too **busy** to come **to us**, we can come **to you** and **pick your dog up**. We **pick up** between the ⁴_____ of **8 and 10 in the morning**. Your **pet** will get a **wash and grooming treatment**, and then enjoy **a walk in the park** with **other dogs** before being ⁵_____ **to your home** in the **afternoon**.

Bow Wow Pet Services is located at **360 West Bridge Street, Norwood**. Phone **557 422 145**. You'll also find us on **Facebook** and **Instagram**.

Bow Wow. Because your **best friend** ⁶_____ the **best possible care!**

B 🎧 Listen again. Are the sentences true or false? Circle **T** for true or **F** for false.

1. Bow Wow Pet Services is a new business.   T / F
2. The pet groomers at Bow Wow also have dogs of their own.   T / F
3. Bow Wow will wash and groom dogs in their owners' homes.   T / F
4. Bow Wow Pet Services is on social media.   T / F

Read the Advertisement Aloud

Now pretend that you are a radio announcer. Read the advertisement for Bow Wow Pet Services aloud. Include the words that you wrote to fill the blanks.

Speak slowly and clearly. Use intonation—stress the important words (make them stronger). Practice by stressing the **bold** words in the advertisement above.

You may practice silently to yourself first. Then read the advertisement aloud to a partner or to your class.

1. _____

2. _____

3. _____

4. _____

5. _____

6. _____

Warm-up

A People do different things in their free time. What are these people doing? Write the name of each activity below the picture.

B Do you do any of these activities in your free time? What other activities do you do? Talk with a partner.

Listening 1

 1-32

A Listen to Takashi speaking with Emma. Answer the questions.

1. Do Emma and Takashi know each other? _____

2. What are they talking about? _____

B Listen again. Check what Takashi and Emma are doing this weekend.

	Takashi	Emma
bike ride	☐	☐
gym	☐	☐
cooking	☐	☐
watch TV	☐	☐

Tips for Communication

Making weekend plans

Takashi and Emma have a conversation about what they are doing at the weekend. Takashi says that he is *looking forward to the weekend*. If you are *looking forward to* something, you are excited about something that will happen in the future.

Takashi invites Emma to join him on a bike ride. He explains what he is planning to do and Emma says *That sounds really good*. We can use *That sounds really good* when we think that an idea or plan that someone is describing is a good idea and we are very interested in it.

Emma says that the best day, for the bike ride for her would be Saturday. Takashi is happy to go on Saturday, and he says *Saturday's fine with me*. We say that something is *fine with me* when we want to agree to a plan or suggestion.

Takashi uses "at some point." *I'm thinking about going for a bike ride **at some point***. This means that he plans to go for a bike ride during the weekend, but he doesn't know when he will do so.

Listening 2

A 🎧 **Listen and write short answers.**

1. Who has been cycling longer? Takashi or Emma? _____

2. When did Emma buy her bike? _____

3. How can Emma sign up for the club? _____

4. Who suggests that they should start riding home? _____

B 🎧 **Listen again. Circle the correct numbers.**

1. Takashi has been cycling since he was about **thirteen** / **fifteen** years old.

2. Takashi usually cycles **thirteen** / **thirty** kilometers on the weekend.

3. Takashi cycles for **fifty** / **sixty** kilometers with the cycling club.

4. It's nearly **five** / **four** o'clock when they start to cycle home.

5. Takashi and Emma have **twenty** / **twenty-five** kilometers to ride home.

Talk with a Partner

👥 **Work with a partner. Take turns to ask and answer about an activity. Use the information in the activity box and the expressions from the language box.**

Activity	How often
cycling	do a thirty-kilometer ride most weekends
playing piano	do a two-hour lesson every week
playing baseball	play a game every weekend
making videos	upload a video on YouTube once a month
Age	**Reason**
ten	I like to keep fit.
eleven	I love playing music.
fifteen	I like to play a team sport.
eighteen	I like to be creative.

LANGUAGE BOX	
A	**B**
How long have you been ...?	I've been ... since I was ... How about you?
I only ... How often do you ...?	I usually ...
What do you like about ...?	It's ...

Grammar Focus

Adverbs of Frequency

Takashi says: *I **usually** do a thirty kilometer ride most weekends. **Sometimes** I go cycling with the club.*

Usually and *sometimes* are adverbs of frequency. We use these adverbs to describe different frequencies. The table below shows frequency expressed as percentages. It is not a definite guide. It is a general guide.

Frequency %	Adverb	Example
100%	always	I **always** study for exams.
90%	usually	I **usually** get up at 7 o'clock.
80%	normally	I **normally** have lunch with friends.
70%	often	I **often** ride my bike to university.
50%	sometimes	I **sometimes** go away for the weekend.
30%	occasionally	I **occasionally** wake up late for class.
10%	seldom	I **seldom** cook for friends.
0%	never	I **never** forget my grandmother's birthday.

Rewrite the sentences with the words in brackets.

1. I study in the library. (often) *I often study in the library.*
2. Pete eats chocolate. (never) _____
3. Sally pays attention in class. (always) _____
4. Tim walks the dog. (sometimes) _____
5. Jo and I study together. (usually) _____

Develop Your Speaking Skills

A Talk with a partner. Take turns to ask and answer about the activities in the table. Ask how often the other person does each activity. Answer using adverbs of frequency. You can add some more activities if you like. Here is an example:

A: How often do you study in the library?
B: I seldom study in the library.

study in the library	forget people's birthdays
cook for friends	eat fish
study for exams	pay attention in class
study with a friend	get up at seven o'clock
wake up late for class	eat chocolate
ride a bike	go away for the weekend

Listening 3: *Recipe*

CD 1-34

A 🎧 Emma is watching a cooking show on TV. Listen and complete the ingredients needed for the recipe.

> INGREDIENTS
> 1. Six _____
> 2. Half a cup of _____
> 3. Two cups of grated _____
> 4. Salt and _____
> 5. A large spoon of _____

B 🎧 Listen again. Number the steps to show the correct order.

> METHOD
> _____ Add the milk   _____ Add some salt and pepper.
> _____ First, beat the eggs.   _____ Heat the butter in a frying pan.
> _____ Add the egg mixture.   _____ Don't let the mixture stick to the frying pan.
> _____ Add the grated cheese.

Listening 4: *Voicemail*

CD 1-35

A 🎧 Listen to the message. Circle the correct answer.

Why is Emma calling Sandra?
a. just for a chat
b. to invite her to a movie
c. to check she is okay

B 🎧 Listen again and circle the correct answers.

1. Which day does Emma mention?
   a. Friday   b. Saturday   c. Sunday
2. What kind of food does Emma mention?
   a. Indian   b. Italian   c. Mexican

Speaking: *Leave a Voicemail Message*

Work with a partner. Take turns to practice leaving a voicemail message about getting together. Use expressions from the box. Use different activities.

> **LANGUAGE BOX**
>
> I'm just calling to see what you're doing this weekend.
> I'm / Donna and I are thinking about going to see a movie on Saturday.
> I'm / We're planning to eat first.
> Do you want to join us? Do you want to come?
> Let me know if you're interested. It would be great to see you.

Music

Warm-up

What kind of music do you like? Classical? Rock? All kinds?

A Look at the list of different kinds of music. There are other kinds, too! Discuss your music likes and dislikes with a partner.

Classical   Jazz   Hip hop

Pop   Rock   Techno

B Look at pictures a–d. Match the words to the pictures.

1. orchestra _____
2. audience _____
3. concert hall _____
4. concert tickets _____

Listening 1

🎧 1-36

A 🎧 **Meg is calling City Concert Hall. Listen and answer the questions.**

1. What is the main purpose of Meg's call?

   a. to reserve concert tickets

   b. to find out about the music that will be played

2. Meg asks two questions. What are they? Check the two questions she asks.

   a. What time does the concert start? ☐

   b. How long will the concert last? ☐

   c. What music will be played? ☐

   d. Is the concert hall wheelchair-accessible? ☐

   e. How can I pay for the tickets? ☐

B 🎧 **Listen again. Circle the correct words.**

1. Meg wants to attend the **afternoon** / **evening** performance.

2. The concert will run for **one hour** / **two hours**.

3. There are wheelchair-accessible parking bays on **Level 1** / **Level 2** of the parking garage.

4. Meg is buying one standard-price ticket and one with the **student** / **senior's** discount.

Tips for Communication

Asking questions in a conversation
Meg says: *But I just have a couple of questions. First, …*
When we are buying something or making arrangements, we sometimes want to let the other person know that we need more information.
Here are some expressions that signal that we are going to ask questions:
I just have a few questions.
I wonder if you can answer a question for me.
There are a few things I'd like to know.
We might then count the questions as we ask them.
First, … The first thing is …   Second, …   And third, …

Listening 2

 1-37

A 🎧 Listen to the conversation between Meg and her grandmother. The concert has just finished. Circle the correct answer.

1. Who is Meg's grandmother's favorite composer?

   a. Bach   **b.** Mozart   **c.** Beethoven

2. What kind of musician do Meg and her grandmother talk about?

   a. a singer   **b.** a guitarist   **c.** a pianist

3. What do Meg and her grandmother do straight after the concert?

   a. go to Meg's grandmother's home

   b. go to the parking garage

   c. go to the café

4. When will they decide to go to their next concert together?

   a. next week   **b.** next month   **c.** next year

B 🎧 Listen again and fill in the blanks.

1. How did you _____ the concert, Grandma?

2. Everything was _____!

3. Well, it's time to go _____.

4. Thank you so much for _____ me to this concert, Meg.

5. You're very _____, Grandma.

Talk with a Partner

👥 Work with a partner. Take turns to ask and answer. Use expressions from the box.

LANGUAGE BOX			
Asking		**Answering**	
She's a good ..., isn't she? He's a good ..., isn't he?	singer guitarist pianist violinist	Yes, she's / he's ...	excellent wonderful brilliant very good

singer

guitarist

pianist

violinist

Grammar Focus

Tag questions

Meg says: *Mozart is your favorite composer, isn't he?* The two words *isn't he?* are a tag question. We can use these when we think that what we are saying is correct and the other person will confirm it. Meg's grandmother answers: *Yes, **he is**.*

Look how we make tag questions with the simple present verb:

Main verb in sentence	Tag	Example	"Yes" answer
is	*isn't* + pronoun	*This **is** a great song, **isn't it**?*	*Yes, **it is**.*
are	*aren't* + pronoun	*They **are** good singers, **aren't they**?*	*Yes, **they are**.*

Complete the tag questions with **isn't** or **aren't**.

1. You're a student, _____ you?
2. Joan is coming to the concert, _____ she?
3. This parking bay is wheelchair-accessible, _____ it?

Develop Your Speaking Skills

A Work in pairs and practice the dialog.

Clerk: How may I help you?
Meg: I would like to purchase two tickets to the Jazz Legends concert tomorrow.
Clerk: Certainly, that's Sunday, June 4. Are you booking for the afternoon or the evening performance?
Meg: The afternoon performance, please. It's at two o'clock, isn't it?
Clerk: Yes, it is. Are you entitled to any discounts?
Meg: Yes, both of us are students.
Clerk: So, two student discount tickets. That's a total of $50

B Now practice. Use these details, and expressions from the box.

Concert name	Date	Times	Standard	Student
Romantic Classics	Sat. June 12	2 p.m., 7 p.m.	$30	$22
Choral Magic	Sun. July 18	1 p.m., 6 p.m.	$25	$20
Cool Country	Sat. May 5	2 p.m., 8 p.m.	$40	$30

LANGUAGE BOX	
Receptionist	**Customer**
How may I help you?	I want to purchase two tickets to ...
Certainly, that's ...	The ... performance, please.
Are you booking for ...?	It's at ..., isn't it?
Are you entitled to any ...?	Yes. Both of us ... / One of us ...

Listening 3: *Short Talk*

🎧 1-38

A 🎧 **You are going to give a short talk about listening to music. First, listen to the model talk below and fill in the blanks.**

Hello, I'm Meg. I'm going to talk to you about the music I like. I have lots of songs downloaded on my ¹_____, so I can listen to music whenever I want to. I listen to it when I'm out walking, when I'm on the bus or train, and even while I'm ²_____. Listening to music helps me to ³_____. I like different ⁴_____ of music. I listen to a lot of pop music, but I also like some ⁵_____ music, and some jazz. I like going to ⁶_____, too.

B Now think about the music you like and how you listen to it. Write your own short talk in the box below. You may use the words or phrases in the language box to help you.

YOUR TALK

LANGUAGE BOX

I'm going to talk to you about ...

I have lots of ...

I listen to it when I'm ...

Listening to music helps me to ... relax / feel good / concentrate ...

I like different kinds of music. I listen to a lot of ..., but I also like some ...

Eating Out

Warm-up

A Different foods have different tastes. We also use many different words to describe how food tastes. What do you think these foods taste like? Do you like the taste of these foods? Talk with a partner.

B Match the words in the box to each of the pictures.

spicy   creamy   oily   salty   sour   sweet

C Read the menu. Complete the definition for each word.

Rosie's Steakhouse

MENU

APPETIZERS	MAIN COURSES	DESSERTS	SIDE DISHES
BBQ chicken wings	*Wagyu* steak	Ice cream	French fries
Garlic prawns	Scotch fillet steak	Chocolate mousse	Salad
Fried mushrooms	T-bone steak	Lemon pudding	Mixed vegetables

1. A(n) _____ _____ is extra food that you eat with the main course.
2. The _____ _____ is the biggest part of the meal.
3. A(n) _____ is something sweet you eat at the end of the meal.
4. A(n) _____ is a small dish that you eat at the beginning of the meal.

Listening 1

CD 1-39

A 🎧 Listen to the conversation.
Write short answers to the questions.

1. Where are they? _____

2. What are they doing? _____

B 🎧 Listen again. What do they order? Write **T** for Tom or **A** for Anna next to the items on the menu.

Appetizers	*Main courses*	*Sides*	*Drinks*
Garlic mushrooms ____	T-bone steak ____	Salad ____	Mineral water ____
BBQ prawns ____	Scotch fillet steak ____	French fries ____	Orange juice ____
	Pasta: ____		Soda ____
	choose from		
	tomato ____		
	cheese ____		
	or cream sauce ____		

Tips for Communication

Ordering at a restaurant

There are some key sentences and phrases that are often used in a restaurant. In the dialog, Anna and Tom are asked what drinks they would like:

Can I *get you something to drink?*

I'd like *some mineral water,* ***please***.

I'll have *some orange juice.*

The waitress checks if they would like to order their food.

Are you ready to order?

When the waitress takes their food order, Anna isn't ready.

I ***haven't*** *decided* ***yet***. *You order first, Tom.*

Then they both give the waitress their order.

Listening 2

 1-40

A 🎧 **Listen to Tom and Anna talking about their food. Circle T for true or F for false.**

1. Tom and Anna are both happy with their main courses.   T / F
2. Tom decides to send his steak back.   T / F
3. Tom is happy with his dessert.   T / F
4. Anna is not happy with her dessert.   T / F

B 🎧 **Listen again. Circle the correct words.**

1. Tom's steak is **hard** / **tough**.
2. Anna's sauce is **creamy** / **yummy**.
3. Anna ordered **lemon cheesecake** / **lemon mousse** for dessert.
4. Tom is **not happy** / **happy** with his dessert.
5. Anna's dessert is a little **sour** / **sweet**.

Talk with a Partner

👥 **Work with a partner. Use the pictures. Take turns to ask about and describe each food. Use expressions from the box in your questions and answers.**

steak

ice cream

fried chicken

lemon cheesecake

LANGUAGE BOX		
Asking about food	**Describing food**	**Describing taste**
How's your ...?	I'm afraid it's been badly cooked.	creamy
Are you enjoying your ...?	It's quite ...	sweet
	It's hard to ...	sour
Is the ... good?	I am enjoying ...	oily
Do you like the ...?	The sauce is very ...	salty
	It's delicious / excellent.	yummy
	It's nice and ... and it's not too ...	spicy
	It's a little ...	bitter
	I'm not really enjoying it.	mild

Grammar Focus

Adjectives and adverbs

When talking about his steak, Tom says: *I'm afraid it's been **badly** cooked.*

In this sentence, *badly* is an adverb. It tells us *how* the steak has been cooked. Tom also says: *The sauce is **nice**, though.*

Nice is an adjective. It describes the sauce.

We can rewrite these two sentences:

I'm afraid it's bad. Bad is an adjective. It describes the steak.

*The sauce is **nicely** cooked. Nicely* is an adverb. It tells us how the sauce is cooked.

Only some adjectives can also be used as adverbs. It is not the case with every adjective. Here are some more examples:

*Sue was **careful** as she washed the cups.   Sue washed the cups **carefully**.*

*The storm was **sudden**.   The storm started **suddenly**.*

*I hope the waiter is **quick**.   The food arrived **quickly**.*

Circle the correct words.

1. Our football team played **bad** / **badly** today.

2. Jack ran **quick** / **quickly** to the park.

3. Erin's illness was **sudden** / **suddenly**.

4. Be **careful** / **carefully**! There is water on the floor.

5. Jeff's injuries are **serious** / **seriously**. He's in hospital.

Develop Your Speaking Skills

You are going to practice describing things using adjectives and adverbs. Take turns with a partner to ask and answer the questions. Use the topics and the adjectives and adverbs below.

How was ...?	It was ...
dinner?	so delicious
Sarah's party?	fun
the English exam?	easy
your holiday in Europe?	very exciting
How was ...?	**It ...**
the basketball game?	played badly
your driving test?	passed easily
Tim's speech?	spoke clearly
the picnic?	rained heavily

Listening 3: *Advertisement*

 1-41

A 🎧 **Listen to the radio advertisement and fill in the blanks.**

Do you love **chicken**? Then **Charlie's Chicken Place** is the place for **you**! Come to **Charlie's Chicken** for ¹_____, **tender fried chicken**. Our **fried chicken** is so ²_____ that our **customers** keep coming back for **more**. Try one of our **fantastic meal deals**. You can have **fried chicken** and ³_____ for **four people** for just **$25**! Yes, that's **$25**! Add one of our **delicious** ⁴_____ dishes for just **$2 each**. Choose from **french fries**, **corn** or **garlic bread**. And **don't forget** our **amazing** ⁵_____. All **desserts** are just **$4.95 each**. **Yes**, that's just **$4.95** for **apple pie**, **chocolate mousse** or **strawberry** ⁶_____. The **choice** is **yours**! Come to **Charlie's Chicken Place** today.

B **Are the sentences true or false? Circle T for true or F for false.**
1. Charlie's Chicken Place just sells chicken. T / F
2. Fried chicken and salad is a meal deal. T / F
3. You can buy fried chicken and salad for five people for $25. T / F
4. The advertisement mentions four side dishes. T / F
5. The desserts cost $4.95 each. T / F

Read the Advertisement Aloud

Now pretend that you are a radio announcer. Read the advertisement for Charlie's Chicken Place aloud. Include the words that you wrote to fill the blanks.

Speak slowly and clearly. Use intonation—stress the important words (make them stronger). Practice by stressing the **bold** words in the advertisement above.

You may practice silently to yourself first. Then read the advertisement aloud to a partner or to your class.

Movies

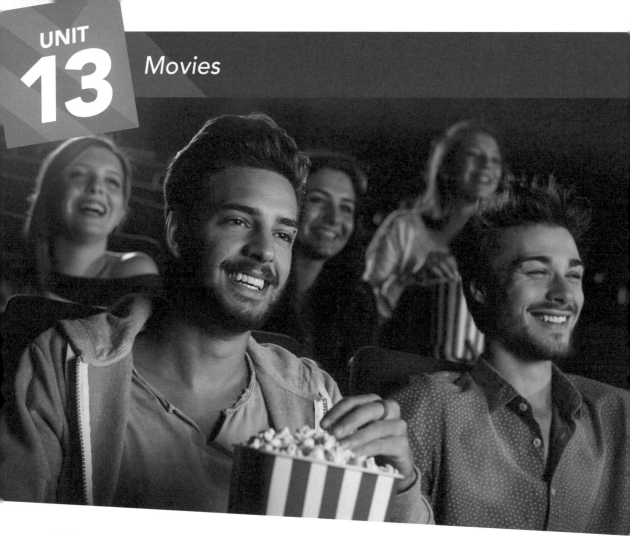

Warm-up

A Talk with a partner. Ask each other these questions.

1. What was the last movie you saw?
2. What was the movie about?
3. Have you ever seen a movie more than once? Which one? Why?

B Look at the mind map of words relating to movies. Check in a dictionary for any words you don't know. Can you add any more words to the mind map?

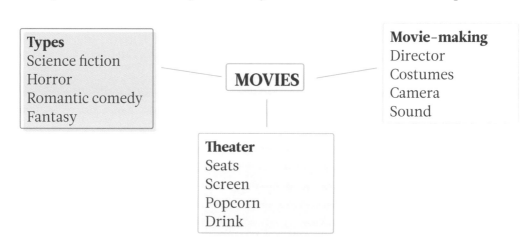

Types
Science fiction
Horror
Romantic comedy
Fantasy

MOVIES

Movie-making
Director
Costumes
Camera
Sound

Theater
Seats
Screen
Popcorn
Drink

Listening 1

 1-42

A 🎧 Listen to Bill speaking with his friend Alex about going to see a movie. Put a circle around the show time of the movie they decide to go to.

Springfield Mall,
River Drive

SPRINGFIELD CINEMA CITY
★ ★ ★ ★ ★

Show times for
Friday 5 August

Die Today, Live Tomorrow
Action, 105 minutes
12:20, 4:30, 7:40   VIEW TRAILER ⟹

Spinning Out
Sci-fi thriller, 95 minutes
1:40, 4:15, 6:30, 8:00   VIEW TRAILER ⟹

Little Dog
Family fun, 80 minutes
12:30, 6:00   VIEW TRAILER ⟹

Call It Off
Romantic comedy, 92 minutes
2:00, 6:15, 8:15   VIEW TRAILER ⟹

B 🎧 Listen again. Answer the questions.

1. Which film does Alex NOT want to see? _____

2. Which film is Chris Stone in? _____

3. Which film are Ryan O'Keefe and Emily Reese in? _____

4. Where is *Spinning Out* set? _____

Tips for Communication

Expressing interest

Talking about a movie, Bill says: *I wouldn't mind seeing that.*

This means he is quite interested in seeing the movie.

We can use the expression *I wouldn't mind* followed by an *-ing* verb to say that we want to do something.

I wouldn't mind getting a bite to eat.

I wouldn't mind meeting up with you for a coffee later today.

Other verbs that often go with *I wouldn't mind* are: *going, having, looking, seeing,* and *coming.*

I wouldn't mind going to the pool later.   I wouldn't mind seeing that movie.

We can also use I *wouldn't mind* followed by a noun to say that we would like to have something. *I wouldn't mind a cup of tea right now.*

Bill and Alex also use these other phrases to express interest in the different movies:

That's a possibility.   That's a maybe.

Let's go to …   I'd be happy to see that.

Listening 2

 1-43

A 🎧 Listen to Bill and Alex discussing the movie *Spinning Out*. They have some different opinions about it. Check **Agree** or **Disagree** for each thing they discuss.

	Agree	Disagree
1. the story	☐	☐
2. the action scenes	☐	☐
3. the music	☐	☐
4. who they would recommend it to	☐	☐

B 🎧 Listen again. Circle the correct words.

1. Alex says he found the story **unbelievable** / **enjoyable**.
2. Alex says the action scenes were **terrible** / **terrific**.
3. Alex says the music was **creepy** / **crazy**.

Talk with a Partner

👥 Work with a partner. Think of a movie you have seen during the past year and give your opinions about it. Use expressions from the box.

LANGUAGE BOX			
Questions	**Opinions**		
What did you think of ...?	I loved it / enjoyed it / didn't like it. I thought the ... was / were ...	story actors music	excellent brilliant funny
Would you recommend it?	I'm definitely going to tell everyone to see it. I don't think it's for everyone.		boring unbelievable interesting

Grammar Focus

The simple past tense: regular and irregular verbs

After Bill and Alex see the movie *Spinning Out*, Bill says: *I **thought** it was exciting. Thought* is the past tense form of the verb *think*.

Alex says: *The music **added** a lot to the movie. Added* is the past tense form of the verb *add*.

Some verbs are regular and some are irregular. The past simple form of regular verbs ends with *-ed*.

Verb	Simple past	Verb	Simple past
walk	walked	enjoy	enjoyed
look	looked	call	called

With irregular verbs, the past simple form does not end with *-ed*. Here are some very common irregular verbs.

Verb	Simple past	Verb	Simple past
be (is, are, am)	was / were	make	made
have	had	see	saw
go	went	say	said

Complete the sentences with a past tense form of one of the verbs above.

1. Tina _____ she was going to be late.

2. We _____ out for dinner after the movie.

3. Jerry and I _____ three movies during the vacation.

Develop Your Speaking Skills

You are going to choose a movie. Work in pairs and practice the dialog.

A: Which movie are we going to see tonight?

B: I'm not sure. Let's look at the cinema website. Okay, there's *Best Friends*.

A: I saw it last week.

B: How about *Run, Danny, Run*?

A: I wouldn't mind seeing that.

B: Then there's *Summer Story*. I've heard it's very good. Let's go to that.

A: Okay, I'd be happy to see that.

LANGUAGE BOX			
Suggesting	**Movie titles**		**Responding**
There's ...	*A Nice Plan*	*Becoming a Star*	I don't want to see that.
There's also ...	*Joey and Meg*	*Galaxy Fighters*	I wouldn't mind ...
Then there's ...	*Flight 33*	*One More Time*	That's a maybe.
How about ...?			I'd be happy to see that.

Listening 3: *Announcement*

 1-44

🎧 Look at the types of TV programs. Then listen to an evening TV program announcement. As you listen, number the types from **1** to **5**.

a. _____ Comedy show

b. _____ Cooking

c. _____ Crime drama

d. _____ News and current affairs

e. _____ Travel

Listening 4: *Voicemail*

 1-45

🎧 **Sue is calling Bill to talk about movies. Listen and circle the correct words.**

1. *Wild and Free* is **three hours** / **ninety minutes** long.

2. Sue likes **the Cineplex** / **the Palace** better.

3. Sue asks Bill to **call her back** / **meet her at the cinema**.

Speaking: *Leave a Voicemail Message*

Work with a partner. Take turns to leave a voicemail message about movie times. Look at the movies, theaters, and times below. Use expressions from the box.

LANGUAGE BOX
Hi ..., it's ... here
Have you decided which movie you want to see tonight?
If we go to ..., it's on at ... and ...
It's a ... movie. / it's ... long.
Or we could see ... at the ...   I think I'd rather see ...
Let me know what you think.   Give me a call back, okay?

High Street Cinema	Movieplex
From Hawaii with Love (90 minutes) 6:30, 8:15	*From Hawaii with Love* (90 minutes) 7:10, 9:00
Where is Sam? (120 minutes) 6:45, 9:15	*Mountain Story* (150 minutes) 6:50

Sport

1. _____

2. _____

3. _____

4. _____

5. _____

6. _____

Warm-up

A Do you play any of these sports? Or do you like to watch any of these sports? Do you play or watch any other sports? Talk with a partner.

B You need special equipment to play most sports. Write the words below the correct picture.

baseball bat / tennis racket / basketball / soccer shoes / table tennis bat / golf club

Listening 1

 1-46

A 🎧 Takashi is talking to Jodie. Answer the questions.

  1. What do Takashi and Jodie talk about?
     a. Saturday night   **b.** baseball

  2. Why does Takashi want Jodie to come to the baseball?
     a. He knows she loves baseball.   **b.** He hasn't seen her recently.

  3. What does Jodie decide to do?
     a. go the baseball   **b.** not go to the baseball

B 🎧 Listen again. Circle the correct words.

  1. Jodie **has** / **has not** been to a baseball game before.
  2. **Jodie** / **Takashi** will buy a ticket.
  3. The friends are meeting at the **stadium** / **station**.
  4. Jodie thanks Takashi for **inviting her** / **buying her a ticket**.

Tips for Communication

Trying to persuade someone

Takashi tries to persuade Jodie to come to the baseball game. He presents different reasons why she should come.

We haven't seen you in a long time.

Yes, Sally's going, and Sam and Tina, too.

Takashi mentions that they haven't seen Jodie in a long time. He hopes that she will decide that it would be nice to see him and his friends. He tells her who is going as another way to make coming to the baseball appealing to Jodie.

Here are some expressions Takashi uses to persuade Jodie:

Come on, it'll be fun!

You'll enjoy it. It's going to be a great game.

If the Saints win, they'll get into the final.

Listening 2

🔊 1-47

A 🎧 Listen to Takashi talking to a manager at the tennis club. Check the topics they talk about.

1. all the sports Takashi plays ☐
2. how many lessons to book ☐
3. cost of lessons ☐
4. membership fee ☐
5. equipment ☐

B 🎧 Listen again. Write short answers to the questions.

1. What kind of lesson should Takashi do first? _____
2. How many lessons do people usually book? _____
3. How much is a one-hour lesson for one person? _____
4. How much is it each year to join the club? _____

Talk with a Partner

👥 You are going to practice asking for and giving information about sports lessons. Use the information in the box below. Work with a partner and take turns to ask and answer about taking lessons for each sport. Use the words and expressions in the language box.

Golf club	Swimming club
Trial lesson Lessons: $60 an hour for one person $80 an hour for two people Membership fee: $150 a year Can hire golf clubs from the club	Lessons: $30 an hour for one person $40 an hour for two people Membership fee: $15 a year

LANGUAGE BOX	
Asking about sports lessons	**Giving information about sports lessons**
I'm thinking about taking ... What are the options if ...? How much are ...? How much is ...? Do I need my own ...?	Have you played ...? I'd probably recommend ... You can book as many ... It's $... an hour ... You have to join ... You'll need ...

Grammar Focus

Conditional sentences

Takashi uses a conditional sentence when he is talking to Jodie about the baseball game: **If the Saints win, they'll get into** the final.

This structure is called the first conditional. In the first conditional, we use

If + present simple verb + *will* + infinitive

We use it to describe things that are likely to happen in the future as a result of something else happening. The Saints reaching the final depends on them winning this game.

Here are some more examples:

If we **run**, **we'll catch** the train.

If you **practice**, **you'll improve** at golf.

If you **email** me, I **won't forget** to book the tickets.

A **Complete the first conditional sentences. Use the verbs in the box.**

> book   see   wake up   catch

1. If you go to bed late, you'll _____ late.
2. If you _____ a trial lesson, you'll learn more about tennis.
3. If you come to the baseball, you'll _____ everyone.
4. If we meet at six o'clock, we'll _____ the 6:10 train.

B **Put the verbs into the correct form, present simple or will + infinitive.**
1. If you _____ (work) hard, you _____ (achieve) good results.
2. If I _____ (learn) how to play tennis, I _____ (join) a club.
3. If we _____ (finish) early, we _____ (catch) the early train.
4. If William's team _____ (win), they _____ (play) in the final.

Develop Your Speaking Skills

You are going to practice making first conditional sentences. Take turns with a partner. Match the words in column A with column B to make sentences.

LANGUAGE BOX		
	A	**B**
If ...	you call me tomorrow,	I'll be tired.
	I see a cheap tennis racket,	we'll be on time for the game.
	we leave now,	you'll need a racket.
	you start to play tennis,	I'll feel more healthy.
	I jog to soccer training,	I'll talk to you then.
	I change my diet,	I'll let you know.

Listening 3: *Short Talk*

CD 1-48

🎧 **You are going to give a short talk about a sport you like to play or watch. First, listen to the model talk below and fill in the blanks.**

Hello, my name is Jessica. I want to tell you about the sport I [1]_____

—soccer. I have been interested in soccer [2]_____ I was five years old. I

became interested in soccer because my [3]_____ used to play. He used to

take me to the park with a ball and we played soccer together. My favorite

[4]_____ is Manchester United. One of the [5]_____ that I love

about soccer is that you don't need much special equipment. All you need is a

[6]_____. I love watching soccer on TV—especially the World Cup.

Speaking

Now think about a sport that you like to play or watch. Write your own short talk in the box below. You may use the words or phrases in the language box to help you.

YOUR TALK

LANGUAGE BOX
I have been interested in ... since ...
I became interested in ... because ...
... used to ...
... always ...
My favorite ...
One of the things that I love ...
I love ...

Warm-up

A Do you know the names of these cities? Have you visited any of them? Which would you like to visit? Why? Talk with a partner.

B Match the words with the correct definition.

1. a must-see	a. exploring an interesting place with an expert
2. recommendations	b. pay to use a car for a short period of time
3. itinerary	c. suggestions
4. guided tour	d. something you really want to see
5. sights	e. a list of things you really want to see or do
6. wish list	f. a list of things to see and do on a trip
7. hire a car	g. interesting things or places to see while visiting

Listening 1

 1-49

A 🎧 Listen to Yoko and Erica. Number the topics from **1** to **5** as you listen.

a. _____ How to get to Washington DC

b. _____ Where to fly home from

c. _____ Where to fly in to first

d. _____ How long to stay in New York

e. _____ Things to do in Los Angeles

B 🎧 Listen again. Complete their itinerary.

TRAVEL ITINERARY: *YOKO & ERICA*

- Fly from Tokyo to **1**_____.
  Stay for **2**_____ days.
- **3**_____ to Washington DC.
  Stay for **4**_____ days.
- **5**_____ to Los Angeles.
  Stay for one **6**_____.
- Fly to **7**_____.

Tips for Communication

Making plans

Making plans with someone involves expressing what you would like to do. Here are some examples from Yoko and Erica's conversation:

I'd really like to *see New York.*

I've always wanted to *go to Washington DC.*

I really want to *go to Los Angeles.*

Both Yoko and Erica express things they would like to do in a way that is not too forceful. If they said **I want to** *go to New York*, it would sound like they may not want to discuss their options.

Yoko and Erica also make suggestions for the trip:

Why don't we *fly to ...?*

I think we'll need ...

I think we should ...

So maybe we should *stay ...*

Let's *fly from ...*

This approach makes the conversation a discussion rather than one person planning the whole trip.

Listening 2

 1-50

🎧 **Listen to the conversation between Yoko and Erica. Circle the correct answer.**

1. Where are they having this conversation?
   a. at the airport
   b. on the subway
   c. in the hotel
2. What kind of advice do they want from the concierge?
   a. where to go
   b. how to get where they are going
   c. where to have dinner
3. What are they doing in Greenwich Village?
   a. shopping
   b. staying in a hotel there
   c. having dinner

Talk with a Partner

👥 **Work with a partner. Talk about the travel itinerary. Use expressions from the box in your questions and answers.**

Itinerary: Los Angeles	Getting around
1. Hollywood Walk of Fame	walk from here to Grauman's Chinese Theatre
2. Grauman's Chinese Theatre	taxi from here to the Hollywood Sign
3. Hollywood sign	taxi from here to Rodeo Drive
4. Rodeo Drive	bus from here to Santa Monica Pier
5. Santa Monica Pier	bus from here to Venice Beach
6. Venice Beach	

LANGUAGE BOX	
Talking about plans	**Talking about getting around**
This morning we're going to ...	I wonder how we get to ...?
Then we're going to explore ...	I think we need to ...
And after that we're going ...	We can walk from / to ...
We're having dinner in ...	We can take ...

Grammar Focus

Definite and indefinite articles

Sometimes we use the definite article *the* and sometimes we use the indefinite article *a*.

This morning we're going to the Metropolitan Museum of Art.

And we can take a taxi back to the hotel from there.

In the first example, we use *the* because there is only one Metropolitan Museum of Art in New York.

In the second example, we use *a* because we do not know exactly which taxi we will take. We can take any taxi.

Complete each sentence using a or the.

1. We can take _____ subway there.
2. Let's catch _____ bus to the restaurant.
3. I'd like to see _____ Empire State Building.
4. I want to go on _____ river cruise.
5. Let's find _____ café and have some coffee.
6. _____ concierge at the hotel is very helpful.

Develop Your Speaking Skills

Read the scenarios below. What would you say in each situation? Take turns with a partner to speak. Use the uncountable nouns you have learned in this section.

1. You are going on vacation with a friend. You need to find a place to stay. You say: *We should …*
2. Tell your friend that you want to visit these places: Statue of Liberty, Hudson River. You say: *I want to visit …*
3. Tell your friend that you want to have lunch. You say: *Let's find …*
4. It's time to go back to the hotel. Taxi is the best way to travel. You say: *I think we should …*
5. You have just finished lunch. You are walking along the street. You can't find your phone. You say: *I think my phone is … restaurant.*
6. You want to make a complaint at the hotel. You say: *I'd like to speak to …*

Listening 3: Advertisement

A 🎧 **Listen to the radio advertisement and fill in the blanks.**

Are you planning a **visit** to **New York**? Make ¹_____ you check

out **Big Apple River Cruises** for the **best cruises** in **New York**. Choose from

²_____ **different cruises** that highlight the **best** that **New York** has to

offer. Our most ³_____ cruise, **New York Highlights**, is on sale with a

20 percent discount for the **next** ⁴_____ **days**. See all the **best sights** on

this cruise; the Empire State Building, the Statue of Liberty, Ellis

⁵_____ and much more. This **cruise** leaves at **10 a.m., 12 p.m.**

and ⁶_____ and is a **90-minute roundtrip**. Our **boats** are **modern,**

comfortable and ⁷_____ and have **free Wi-Fi**. Enjoy the **views** from

outside or inside. Have a **meal or snack** in our **excellent** ⁸_____.

We have been running **New York river cruises** for ⁹_____ **years**.

You will not regret taking a **Big Apple river cruise**. Visit our **website** at **www.**

bigapplerivercruise.com to **find out more** or make a ¹⁰_____.

B **Are the sentences true or false? Circle T for true or F for false.**

1. Many people choose the New York Highlights cruise.   T / F
2. The New York Highlights cruise leaves twice a day.   T / F
3. You can eat on the boat.   T / F
4. Big Apple Cruises is a new company.   T / F

Read the Advertisement Aloud

Now pretend that you are a radio announcer. Read the advertisement for Big
Apple River Cruises aloud. Include the words that you wrote to fill the blanks.

Speak slowly and clearly. Use intonation—stress the important words (make them
stronger). Practice by stressing the **bold** words in the radio advertisement above.

You may practice silently to yourself first. Then read the advertisement aloud to a
partner or to your class.

TEXT PRODUCTION STAFF

edited by	編集
Yasutaka Sano	佐野 泰孝
Minako Hagiwara	萩原 美奈子
English–language editing by	英文校閲
Bill Benfield	ビル・ベンフィールド
cover design by	表紙デザイン
Nobuyoshi Fujino	藤野 伸芳
text design by	本文デザイン
ALIUS	アリウス

CD PRODUCTION STAFF

narrated by	吹き込み者
Chris Koprowski (AmerE)	クリス・コプロスキ (アメリカ英語)
Karen Haedrich (AmerE)	カレン・ヘドリック (アメリカ英語)
Dominic Allen (AmerE)	ドミニク・アレン (アメリカ英語)
Erica Williams (AmerE)	エリカ・ウィリアムズ (アメリカ英語)

Listen Up, Talk Back Book 1 —English for Everyday Communication—
聞いて話せる英語演習 Book 1—頻出表現で学ぶ実用英語—

2020年1月20日　初版発行
2023年2月25日　第4刷発行

著　　者　Gillian Flaherty
　　　　　James Bean
　　　　　鎌倉　義士

発 行 者　佐野 英一郎
発 行 所　株式会社 成美堂
　　　　　〒101-0052　東京都千代田区神田小川町3-22
　　　　　TEL 03-3291-2261　FAX 03-3293-5490
　　　　　https://www.seibido.co.jp

印刷・製本　萩原印刷株式会社

ISBN 978-4-7919-7204-3　　　　　　　　　　　　　Printed in Japan